God's Gift of Sexuality

Younger Youth Guide
Revised Edition

God's Gift of Sexuality

A Study for Young People in the Presbyterian Church (U.S.A.)

Younger Youth Guide
Revised Edition

Writers

Janet Bartosch
Woody Berry
Eleanor Cammer
Janet Ollila Colberg
Carol Hunter-Geboy
Diane Maodush-Pitzer
Paul M. Thompson
Rebecca Voelkel-Haugen
Linda Woodard

Editor

Mary Lee Talbot

Editor for Revised Edition

David M. Dobson

Witherspoon Press
Louisville, Kentucky

© 1989 Presbyterian Publishing House

© 1998 Witherspoon Press, Presbyterian Church (U.S.A.), Louisville, Kentucky

Scripture quotations (unless otherwise identified) are from the New Revised Standard Version of the Bible, copyright 1989 by the Division of Christian Education of the National Council of the Churches of Christ in the U.S.A., and are used by permission. In some instances, language has been changed for inclusivity.

Editor: Mary Lee Talbot

Editor for Revised Edition: David M. Dobson

Editorial Assistants: Connie Ellis and Ruth Ann Burks

Art Director: Anthony Feltner

Cover Design: Anthony Feltner

Illustrations: Bud Hixson

Revised edition

Published by Witherspoon Press, a Ministry of the General Assembly Council, Congregational Ministries Division, Presbyterian Church (U.S.A.), Louisville, Kentucky

PRINTED IN THE UNITED STATES OF AMERICA

98 99 00 01 02 03 04 05 06 07 — 10 9 8 7 6 5 4 3 2 1

Web site address: http://www.pcusa.org/pcusa/witherspoon

ISBN 1-57895-062-7

Contents

Preface to the Revised Edition

The numbers are staggering.

In the nine years since this course was introduced, nearly eight million teenage Americans became pregnant. More than twenty million teens acquired some type of sexually transmitted infection. And more than 500,000 cases of AIDS were diagnosed; many of those diagnosed most likely acquired the disease as teens.

We live in a culture that constantly bombards its young people with confusing messages about sex and sexuality. Sex is everywhere: in the advertisements aimed at our children, in the television shows and movies they watch, in the music they listen to. But the media and popular culture can't be blamed for everything. We as parents and educators have to take some responsibility for too often standing on the sidelines as the numbers grow: by age 15, one in four girls and one in three boys are sexually active; by age 20, four out of five young Americans have had sexual intercourse; HIV/AIDS is increasing in the heterosexual population, especially among young women; and the number of teen pregnancies shows no signs of decreasing.

But there is reason for hope. AIDS awareness and education has improved dramatically in the 1990s; sex education is now the rule rather than the exception in our public schools; ratings systems are helping parents decide what is appropriate for their children to watch on television; and after a public outcry, a prominent fashion company was forced to cancel advertisements featuring youth in sexually suggestive situations.

The Presbyterian Church (U.S.A.) has not stood by silently either. This course for youth and older youth was created in response to a mandate from the General Assembly. And in 1996, a sexuality education curriculum for elementary-age children and their parents was produced, also in response to a General Assembly mandate.

There are the numbers, but there is also hope. This course is part of that hope.

Preface to the First Edition

This course is a response to an action of the 195th General Assembly (1984) of the Presbyterian Church (U.S.A.) and a response to all who are concerned for young people today. The former Youth and Young Adult Staff Team and Third World Women's Coordinating Committee of the Program Agency began this project. It has been completed by the Education and Congregational Nurture Ministry Unit. Developmental money for *God's Gift of Sexuality* came from Presbyterian Women through the Women's Opportunity Giving Fund, which is one of the predecessors to the Creative Ministries projects of Presbyterian Women.

This course is made up of four sections: a leader's guide, a book for parents, a book for younger youth, and a book for older youth. It is designed to be used in church retreat settings. The course uses the Scripture and the church doctrine, as well as activities from a variety of sources, to help young people put sexuality into a Christian perspective.

In its development this course has doubly benefited from the wisdom of a task force and the willingness of fifty congregations in the Presbyterian Church (U.S.A.) to test the course with their young people and parents. Their help has been invaluable.

The task force, the authors, and the editor hope that this course will help the young people of our denomination to develop a healthy Christian attitude toward their sexuality.

About the Writers

Janet Bartosch is a family nurse practitioner with a master's of science in nursing and a master's of education in community health. She has extensive clinical experience in women's health and has offered workshops for parents and teens on sexuality. She has published for professional journals, is currently employed as a medical software editor, and contracts her services as a nurse practitioner. She is the mother of two teenage boys.

The Rev. Woody Berry is pastor of Webster Presbyterian Church, Webster, Texas. He has served as an ordained minister for twenty years in congregations in Texas and Colorado and has been active in educational leadership events across the denomination. He received his bachelor's degree at the University of Texas and master of divinity and doctor of ministry degrees from Austin Presbyterian Theological Seminary. He was coauthor of the Presbyterian Church (U.S.A.) sexuality curriculum for children, *God's Plan for Growing Up*, as well as other church curricula. He has been married for more than twenty-five years to Jan Berry, and they have two teenage children, a daughter, Kennedy, and a son, Christopher.

Eleanor Cammer is a certified Presbyterian Christian educator for Vienna Presbyterian Church in Vienna, Virginia. She has an M.R.E. from Wesley Theological Seminary in Washington, D.C., and is also a certified Human Sexuality Educator. In 1996, she delivered a lecture on "The History of Sexuality," as part of the Smithsonian Lecture Series. She is married, with three daughters and six grandchildren.

Janet Ollila Colberg has worked as a high school nurse for twenty years in Helena, Montana. She and her husband Steve and son Josh are members of the First Presbyterian Church of Helena. Her son Jason and daughter-in-law Laura are active in the Presbyterian Church and Youth Fellowship in Seattle. Janet's master's degree is in counseling. She has written two books and several papers on youth health and sexuality issues, including the book *Red Light, Green Light: Preventing Teen Pregnancy*. She is the 1997–98 Montana School Nurse of the Year.

Carol Hunter-Geboy has her Ph.D. in developmental psychology and has taught sexuality education for more than twelve years. She has trained more than eight thousand people in thirty-five states to work with young people on issues of sexuality education. She has developed curricula for a variety of national organizations including the Salvation Army, Girls Clubs of America, and the Center for Population Options. She currently works for the American Red Cross on issues concerning sexuality.

The Rev. Diane Maodush-Pitzer is the founding director of Witness—a nonprofit ecumenical center of mentoring, advocacy, and support that works toward the transformation of the church through the witness of women so that men and women, as equal partners, may participate fully in the ministry of Jesus Christ. Ordained in the Reformed Church in America, Diane regularly lectures, teaches, and writes in the area of sexuality, education, and liturgy. Along with her husband, Diane is the parent of three young boys and lives in Grand Rapids, Michigan.

The Rev. Dr. Paul M. Thompson is an interim pastor in the Dallas area and is a licensed professional counselor in private practice. He has taught parenting and sexuality education courses for youth and adults in churches throughout the country for more than twenty years. He is the author of *The Giving Book*, a resource for youth ministry. Paul's wife Terri is a middle school principal, and they have four children.

The Rev. Rebecca Voelkel-Haugen is the pastor of Spirit of the Lakes United Church of Christ. Before that she was a program staff member at the Center for the Prevention of Sexual and Domestic Violence. She is coauthor of *Sexual Abuse Prevention: A Course of Study for Teenagers*, published by United Church Press. Rebecca lives with her partner Kris in Minneapolis.

The Rev. Linda Woodard is a pastor in Rome, Georgia. She has led courses on sexuality education at the Montreat Youth Conference and the Youth Triennium. She began teaching in this subject area through her work with the United Methodist Church sex education program.

About the Editors

David M. Dobson is an acquisitions editor for Bridge Resources and Witherspoon Press, two imprints of Curriculum Publishing, Presbyterian Church (U.S.A.). He is a member of the National Council of Churches Committee on Family Ministry and Human Sexuality. He and his wife Myriam, a Montessori educator, have two children and are members of Highland Presbyterian Church in Louisville, Kentucky.

The Rev. Mary Lee Talbot served on the Youth and Young Adult Staff Team of the Program Agency from 1981 to 1988. She is the writer and/or editor of a number of youth ministry resources. She received her Ph.D. from Columbia University Teachers College in New York City. Currently, she serves as director of Continuing Education and Special Events at Pittsburgh Theological Seminary.

A Reformed/Presbyterian Understanding of Sexuality

Our essential affirmation is that God is a God of love who comes to us, offering us the gift of a new and meaningful life through Jesus Christ. We know and understand who God is through Jesus and can best know Christ through Scripture and through its interpretation by the church. We believe that God has given us God's Spirit to enliven and empower us to be God's followers in the world. We believe that our lives are to be used in thanksgiving to God by loving God, one another, and ourselves.

Thus a Reformed/Presbyterian understanding of sexuality begins with a belief in a God of love who has created us as sexual beings to relate to one another in love. We believe in educating young people so they can learn about all aspects of sexuality, including the physical aspects, the emotional aspects, the beliefs and values we hold that inform our sexuality, and the appropriate ways to make decisions about our sexuality. All of this knowledge helps us live out our sexuality in love and thanksgiving to God.

We begin the explanation of our understanding of sexuality with the Bible. The Bible is our basic textbook because it describes God's faithfulness to us. Some things we need to remember about our biblical faith include the following:

1. We believe in a personal, transcendent God who is the self-sufficient Sovereign of all being. Based on God's attributes of justice, righteousness, holiness, and love, God determines what is right and just in creation.

2. Through the law in the Old and New Testaments, God has specified what is right and wrong. All of God's commands undergird and reinforce the objective moral universe. God holds us accountable as moral stewards of creation.

3. Men and women are unique as God's image bearers. Like God, we are personal, moral, and spiritual beings, capable of an intimate relationship with God and with other human beings.

4. Christian ethics founded on biblical principles will try to avoid the following dangers: legalism (belief that Scripture is merely a rule book containing moral proof texts); situationalism (belief that there are no moral absolutes but that situations dictate what is right and wrong); and intuitionism (belief that moral knowledge is an exclusively internal and subjective experience).

5. A biblical ethic on human sexuality needs to include the following precepts:

a. Norms or standards are revealed by God in Scripture. In every situation we must ask, What does the Bible teach?

b. Situations in history progress under God's guidance. In every situation we must ask, What would honor God?

c. Existential motivation is prompted by the Holy Spirit. In every situation we must ask, How do I (we) respond?

We are forgiven sinners, and, guided by the Holy Spirit, we can use our sexuality as God intended. Norms, context, and motivation are essential to moral Christian sexual activity.

This course is based on seven biblical and theological principles that provide the guidance and support for understanding our sexuality. These affirmations are the following:

1. God created us and gave us the gift of our sexuality.

2. God created us for life in community.

3. Our church is a community of love.

4. Our church is a community of responsibility.

5. Our church is a varied community.

6. Our church is a community of forgiveness.

7. God gives us responsibility for our own decisions.

Each of the foregoing theological affirmations is highlighted in this section. In standard Reformed/Presbyterian fashion, each affirmation begins with Scripture, is followed with a quotation from a theological document, and is then briefly explained in language meaningful to a young person. Use these affirmations to set the stage for understanding our sexuality, and post them in a prominent place to remind your young people of the strong and positive guidance the church provides for them. These theological affirmations have also been included in the guides for the young people to help them understand and apply these values and beliefs in their decision making about the use of their sexuality.

We have stated the theological affirmations in a positive way. Sexuality is a good and positive part of our lives as intended by God. In order for our sexuality to be a good part of our lives, it must be used responsibly.

To belong to the church means to share in the values of the church. On the one hand, we have boundaries; on the other hand, we must each make decisions for ourselves. Thus, within the community, there is room for us to move about. This freedom allows for the variety that exists within the Reformed/Presbyterian family.

The guiding principles that define our community are love, responsibility, and forgiveness. Within the boundaries of the church, there is freedom, but this freedom is bounded by love and responsibility. There is always the possibility of the irresponsible use of our sexuality. When this happens, we are still a part of the church and are called to confession and forgiveness within the bounds of the church.

We hope that young people in the Reformed/ Presbyterian churches can grow to appreciate the wonderful gift of human sexuality God has given them and will be able to make a good, healthy, and hopeful affirmation about their own sexuality.

God Created Us and Gave Us the Gift of Our Sexuality

> Then God said, "Let us make humankind in our image, according to our likeness; and let them have dominion over . . . the earth." So God created humankind in [God's] image, in the image of God [God] created them; male and female [God] created them. . . . God saw everything that [God] had made, and indeed, it was very good.
>
> (Gen. 1:26, 27, 31a)

> For we are what [God] has made us, created in Christ Jesus for good works.
>
> (Eph. 2:10)

> God made human beings male and female for their mutual help and comfort and joy. We recognize that our creation as sexual beings is part of God's loving purpose for us. God intends all people . . . to affirm each other as males and females with joy, freedom, and responsibility.
>
> ("A Declaration of Faith," ch. 2, lines 80–84, 87–88)

> God has created . . . male and female and given them a life which proceeds from birth to death in a succession of generations and in a wide complex of social relations. . . . Life is a gift to be received with gratitude and a task to be pursued with courage.
>
> (The Confession of 1967, 9.17)

God created us and called us very good. God did not create us as spirits. God did not create us as bodies. Instead, God created us as total persons—body and spirit. And this entire creation, God called very good.

Not only did God create us, but God created us to be God's very own image in the world. All that we are—including our bodies, including our sexuality—is God's gift to us.

Our sexuality is our way of being male or female in the world. Our sexuality is basic and affects our thoughts, feelings, and actions. Because our sexuality is called good by God, because it is God's gift to us, and because we are made in the image of God, we can feel good about our sexuality.

God Created Us for Life in Community

> Owe no one anything, except to love one another; for the one who loves another has fulfilled the law. The commandments, "You shall not commit adultery; You shall not murder; You shall not steal; You shall not covet"; and any other commandment, are summed up in this word, "Love your neighbor as yourself." Love does no wrong to a neighbor; therefore, love is the fulfilling of the law.
>
> (Rom. 13:8–10)

> God made us for life in community.
>
> ("A Declaration of Faith," ch. 2, line 61)

> The new life takes shape in a community in which men and women know that God loves them and accepts them in spite of what they are.
>
> (The Confession of 1967, 9.22)

God created us to be together. From the very beginning, God's purpose was for us to be together—with God and with one another.

One word to define this togetherness is "relationship." A *relationship* is how we describe the connection between two people. The connection might be the result of birth; we have particular relationships with our parents and brothers and sisters. The connection might be the result of feelings and commitments; we have particular relationships with acquaintances, friends, and partners. God creates us with a basic need to form relationships with others. Our relationships are answers to the loneliness we feel, and they give our lives meaning.

Another word to define this togetherness that God has in mind for us is "community." A *community* is a group of people who join together with one another. You are a part of many communities—your neighborhood, your town or city, your own particular group of friends, your church. God created us to be together in communities, which can give meaning and identity to our lives.

The very heart of what it means to be in the image of God is to be in community—joined with God and with one another. When we gather in God's name, we are God's community, the church, in the world. In the church we learn to be who God created us to be. We find our true identity with God and one another in the church.

Our Church Is a Community of Love

> Beloved, let us love one another, because love is from God; everyone who loves is born of God and knows God. Whoever does not love does not know God, for God is love. . . . Beloved, since God loved us so much, we also ought to love one another. No one has ever seen God; if we love one another, God lives in us, and God's love is perfected in us.
>
> (1 John 4:7–8; 11–12)

> And one of them, a lawyer, asked [Jesus] a question to test him. "Teacher, which commandment in the law is the greatest?" He said to him, " 'You shall love the Lord your God with all your heart, and with all your soul, and with all your mind.' This is the greatest and first commandment. And a second is like it: 'You shall love your neighbor as yourself.' On these two commandments hang all the law and the prophets."
>
> (Matt. 22:35–40)

> Q. 42. What is the sum of the Ten Commandments?

A. The sum of the Ten Commandments is: to love the Lord our God with all our heart, with all our soul, with all our strength, and with all our mind; and our neighbor as ourselves.

(The Shorter Catechism, 7.042)

We are created to be in community, in relationship, with God and with one another. Above all else, God has loved us, does love us, and will love us faithfully. In the same way, we should love God and one another.

The summation of the law by Jesus—to love God and to love your neighbor as yourself—indicates that the love of oneself is included in the love of others. Clearly our sexual attitudes and relationships should be motivated by love both for our neighbors and for ourselves. Our sense of identity and our way of acting should affirm others as well as affirm ourselves and should respect others as well as respect ourselves. We are to be concerned for others' needs and feelings without discounting our own.

Because we are total persons, we express our maleness or femaleness in all our relationships. Physical intimacy progresses from the simple affirmation of a handshake or hug to the total intimacy of marriage. Different levels of physical intimacy are appropriate to different kinds and stages of relationships. Often in a relationship, we find ourselves asking what is appropriate. One way to determine the appropriateness of the physical expression of our sexuality is by evaluating the level of committed and faithful love in the relationship.

Our Church Is a Community of Responsibility

The fruit of the Spirit is love, joy, peace, patience, kindness, generosity, faithfulness, gentleness, and self-control.

(Gal. 5:22–23a)

[God] has told you . . . what is good; and what does the Lord require of you but to do justice, and to love kindness, and to walk humbly with your God?

(Micah 6:8)

We believe that we have been created to relate to God and each other in freedom and responsibility.

We may misuse our freedom and deny our responsibility by trying to live without God and other people or against God and other people.

Yet we are still bound to them for our life and well-being, and intended for free and responsible fellowship with them.

("A Declaration of Faith," ch. 2, lines 66–73)

The Church, as the household of God, is called to lead men [and women] out of this [sexual] alienation into the responsible freedom of the new life in Christ. Reconciled to God, each person has joy in and respect for his [or her] own humanity and that of other persons.

(The Confession of 1967, 9.47)

Sexuality is a good and positive part of our lives created by God. In order for our sexuality to continue to be a good part of our lives, it must be used responsibly. Some people define responsible sexuality by saying that certain actions are wrong and others are right and that responsible behavior is simply a matter of following these rules. At the other extreme, some say deciding for yourself what is right and wrong is an individual matter.

Our understanding of responsible sexuality is not found at these two extremes. We are a part of a community of faith. Joined together, we read and study God's Word, pray and listen for God's guidance for us, study the beliefs of our church in the past, and then, being guided by all this, we make statements together that express our beliefs. Presbyterians do take definite stands on issues. At the same time, we uphold the right of each person to maintain the dignity of his or her own conscience in the light of Scripture.

To belong to the church means to share in the values of the church. The guiding principle that defines the church is love. Within the boundaries of the church, there is freedom, but this freedom is bounded by love. We are free to use our sexuality, and yet we are limited in this freedom because of our commitment to God to live a life of love and obedience. We care about the effects of our actions on others as well as on ourselves. Therefore, our sexuality is to be expressed lovingly, responsibly, and obediently.

We know we are expressing our sexuality lovingly, responsibly, and obediently when we work for love and justice in the world. We also know that God's Spirit is present when there is love, joy, peace, patience, kindness, goodness, fidelity, gentleness, and self-control. We can be sure that we are acting responsibly when we keep God's Spirit as the guide of our lives.

Our Church Is a Varied Community

> For just as the body is one and has many members, and all the members of the body, though many, are one body, so it is with Christ. For in the one Spirit we were all baptized into one body—Jews or Greeks, slaves or free—and we are all made to drink of one Spirit. . . . Now you are the body of Christ and individually members of it.
>
> (1 Cor. 12:12–13, 27)

> There is no longer Jew or Greek, there is no longer slave or free, there is no longer male and female; for all of you are one in Christ Jesus.
>
> (Gal. 3:28)

> The young need to see in the church role models of both sexes who communicate by life, even more than by words, the goodness of our femaleness and maleness and the equal opportunity of both for service, responsibility, and authority in the life of the church. They need to see the varied responsible ways in which one can live out one's maleness and femaleness and be helped to affirm the goodness of their own sexuality.
>
> ("The Nature and Purpose of Human Sexuality," lines 469–475)

The many ways in which people choose to live out their relationships include casual acquaintances, friendship, and marriage. In all our relationships we are to relate to one another lovingly and responsibly.

Some people remain single all their lives. They have friendships and close loving relationships without necessarily having sexual intercourse. Sometimes people are widowed or divorced and must renew friendships and other relationships as a single person. Marriage is a covenant of love and responsibility in which a couple makes a commitment of faithfulness. Sexual intercourse is the ultimate expression of this mutual and lasting covenant. Some people choose to become parents, making commitments to love, protect, and support their children.

The ways we live out our relationships are influenced by many factors: our families, our friends, our early sexual experiences, and the sex education we receive. Other factors that influence us are the particular economic, racial, and ethnic group to which we belong and the community in which we live. Sometimes we live out our relationships in sexist ways—stereotyping males and females in particular ways and assigning them superior or inferior status simply because they are males or females. Sometimes we live out our relationships in racist ways—stereotyping particular groups of people simply because of their race or ethnicity. In our own church, we have held and sometimes still hold sexist and racist views. To avoid these views, we must embrace the diversity within our community and strive toward a good, positive, and healthy view of our sexuality as God has intended.

Whether we are children, youth, or adults; single, divorced, married, or widowed; male or female; heterosexual or homosexual; and whatever our economic status or racial/ethnic heritage, we are all loved by a God who is faithful and just.

Our Church Is a Community of Forgiveness

> Do not judge, and you will not be judged; do not condemn, and you will not be condemned. Forgive, and you will be forgiven; give, and it will be given to you. A good measure, pressed down, shaken together, running over, will be put into your lap; for the measure you give will be the measure you get back.
>
> (Luke 6:37–38)

When we fail each other as parents or partners, we are called to forgive each other as God forgives us and to accept the possibilities for renewal that God offers us in grace.

("A Declaration of Faith,"
ch. 2, lines 106–109)

The church comes under the judgment of God and invites rejection by [people] when it fails to lead men and women into the full meaning of life together, or withholds the compassion of Christ from those caught in the moral confusion of our time.

(The Confession of 1967, 9.47)

We have all misused our sexuality. There are times when we have not used our sexuality responsibly. There are times when we have not been grateful for the gift of our sexuality. There are times when we all have fallen short of the high calling God has for us, including the use of our sexuality. This is called sin. When this happens, we are still a part of the church and called to confession and forgiveness within the bounds of the church.

We can be grateful that the church is a community of forgiven people, not an exclusive circle of the morally pure. In our church, we can honestly acknowledge our sins. God's forgiveness makes such honesty possible and helps us to change our lives to reflect God's love. God's Holy Spirit enables us to change and guides us. Rather than rejection and condemnation because we have fallen short of God's intention and our own best aspirations, in the church we can experience forgiveness and receive help in living out our sexuality. We are then all the more willing to forgive the failings of others because we have experienced God's love in such abundance.

God Gives Us Responsibility for Our Own Decisions

I appeal to you therefore, brothers and sisters, by the mercies of God, to present your bodies as a living sacrifice, holy and acceptable to God, which is your spiritual worship. Do not be conformed to this world, but be transformed by the renewing of your minds, so that you may discern what is the will of God—what is good and acceptable and perfect.

(Rom. 12:1–2)

If the people of the church are to be given the resources to live out their lives responsibly as sexual beings, the enabling leadership of the church must . . . assist people in their problems of identity and moral choice. This assistance will, however, have deprived people of the chance to grow and of the need to wrestle with their own choices if it consists predominantly of handing out prescriptions and passing judgment. What is more, the counsel of the church will be sought more if people see in its stance not only a convinced perspective that orients its approach but also a willingness to recognize the complexity of sexual problems, the possibility of conscientious disagreement on moral decisions, and the opportunity for renewal of life for forgiven sinners.

("The Nature and Purpose of
Human Sexuality," lines 689–700)

In our decision making, we are instructed by God's Word to us. We are to be influenced by our Christian beliefs. We are aware of other influences: what our friends believe, how we feel, and what we have learned about our sexuality. We need to learn to sort out those different factors, because some may be sexist, racist, or the result of pressures from others.

The guiding principles that define the church are love, responsibility, obedience, and forgiveness. Keeping these principles in mind and exploring their meanings within our community will lead us to make responsible decisions for our own lives.

To talk about how we make decisions for ourselves and how we communicate those decisions to others is important. Our decisions, based on love, responsibility, and forgiveness, are discovered in relationship with God, with one another, and with ourselves.

Guide for the Presbyterian Church (U.S.A.)

Each year the Presbyterian Church (U.S.A.) meets in a General Assembly of commissioners, comprised of clergy and elders, who gather to address the issues before the church. At these meetings, issues of moral and social concern are often discussed. The Assembly sometimes will appoint committees to study the issues and report back. The Assembly can then endorse these studies with recommended actions it believes should be taken.

These statements are then sent to the whole church. Their purpose is to speak to the church on the particular issues. They are meant as guides to help us in understanding the issues. They are meant to provoke our own thinking. They can help us understand and grow in our faith. These statements are not used as an official pronouncement of what Presbyterians believe. Although they are not binding on the conscience of any member of the Presbyterian Church (U.S.A.), they do help us understand the boundaries of our community.

This guide is compiled from the Scriptures and from several documents that have been endorsed as setting forth the understandings of recent General Assemblies. Included also are statements from *The Book of Confessions*. The guide is in the form of questions and answers that should be helpful to young people in the church. The guide is written in language meaningful to a layperson, so please refer to the original document as reprinted in the Minutes of the General Assembly for more thorough information or for issues of interpretation.

List of Topics for Definition and Discussion

Human Sexuality

Equality of Men and Women

Marriage

Procreation and Contraception

Infertility

Premarital Sex

Extramarital Sex

Sexual Abstinence

Masturbation

Divorce

Abortion

Homosexuality

Sexual Misconduct

Decision Making

Documents Cited

Document 1: The Second Helvetic Confession, from *The Book of Confessions*.

Document 2: The Confession of 1967, from *The Book of Confessions*.

Document 3: "Sexuality and the Human Community," a study document adopted by the 182nd General Assembly, PCUS (1970).

Document 4: "A Declaration of Faith," a study document adopted by the 117th General Assembly (1977) of the Presbyterian Church in the United States.

Document 5: "The Church and Homosexuality," a study document adopted by the 190th General Assembly, UPCUSA (1978), as reprinted in the Minutes of the 198th General Assembly PC(USA) (1986).

Document 6: "Homosexuality and the Church: A Position Paper," a study document adopted by the 119th General Assembly, PCUS (1979), as reprinted in the Minutes of the 198th General Assembly, PC(USA) (1986).

Document 7: "Marriage—A Theological Statement," a study document adopted by the 120th General Assembly, PCUS (1980).

Document 8: "The Nature and Purpose of Human Sexuality," a study document adopted by the 120th General Assembly, PCUS (1980).

Document 9: "The Covenant of Life and the Caring Community," a study document adopted by the 195th General Assembly, UPCUSA (1983).

Document 10: "Covenant and Creation: Theological Reflections on Contraception and Abortion," a study document adopted by the 195th General Assembly, UPCUSA (1983).

Document 11: Policy Statements and Recommendations of the 197th General Assembly (1985). Assembly Committee on Justice and the Rights of Persons.

Document 12: "A Brief Statement of Faith," from *The Book of Confessions.*

Document 13: Report of the Assembly Committee on General Assembly Council Review, adopted by the 206th General Assembly, PC(USA) (1994), as printed in the Minutes of the 206th General Assembly, pp. 86–90.

Document 14: "Do Justice, Love Mercy, Walk Humbly," report of the Special Committee on Problem Pregnancies and Abortion, adopted by the 204th General Assembly, PC(USA) (1992), as printed in the Minutes of the 204th General Assembly, pp. 357–377.

Document 15: Overture adopted by the 207th General Assembly, PC(USA) (1995), as printed in the Minutes of the 207th General Assembly, pp. 678–679.

Document 16: Resolution of the 205th General Assembly, PC(USA) (1993), as printed in the Minutes of the 205th General Assembly, pp. 118–119.

Document 17: Policy statement adopted by the 203rd General Assembly, PC(USA) (1991), as printed in the Minutes of the 203rd General Assembly, pp. 76–92.

Human Sexuality

Why Were We Created as Sexual Beings?

We were created as sexual beings so that we could be in relationships and community with one another and with God. Our sexuality allows for intimacy and allows us to be co-creators with God (Doc. 8, pp. 7, 11). See also Gen. 1:27–31; 2:18–25.

Were We Created as Sexual Beings for the Purpose of Procreation?

We are sexual beings, first, for the purpose of relating to one another, and second, for the purpose of procreation (Doc. 8, p. 7). See also Gen. 2:18–35.

In What Ways Should We Express Our Sexuality?

Our sexuality should be expressed in ways that are loving, self-expressive, creative, faithful, sensitive to the needs of others, honest, self-giving, socially responsible, joyful, and patient (Doc. 8, p. 11). See also Gen. 5:22–23.

When Do We Become Sexual Beings?

We are sexual beings from the moment of creation. No matter the age, state of development, or level of health, we are all sexual beings (Doc. 8, p. 3; Doc. 7, lines 79–88). See also Gen. 1:27–31.

What Is the Relationship between Sex and Love?

One's sexual attitudes and relationships should be motivated by unconditional care both for one's neighbor and oneself (Doc. 8, p. 10). See also Matt. 22:35–40; Luke 10:25–28; 1 Cor. 10:24–33.

What Is Our Church's Role in Developing Understanding of Sexuality?

First of all, the leadership of our church must be educated concerning sexuality. Second, we should not merely hand out prescriptions or pass judgment. Instead, we must recognize how complex our sexuality is, that we disagree in our understandings, and that there is always the need for forgiveness. Third, we should be clear about what we believe, but not speak as if we are sinless. Instead, we should see ourselves as fellow learners, trying to live responsibly with one another (Doc. 8, p. 18; Doc. 2, para. 9.47). See also Rom. 3:21–26.

Does Our Church Advocate Sex Education in the Schools?

We support sexuality education programs in families, churches, schools, and private and public agencies (Doc. 10, p. 60).

Equality of Men and Women

In the Genesis 2 Creation Story, Woman Is Created After Man. Does This Mean Woman Is Subordinate to Man?

No, woman is not subordinate, but rather, she completes Creation. She is created in equality and solidarity with man (Doc. 8, p. 7). See also Gen. 1:27–31; 2:18–25.

How Is the Equality of Men and Women Understood in Old Testament Times?

Male domination and male-centeredness were the norm, although there were exceptions, such as the following: (1) women took active roles in the liberation of the Hebrews from Egypt; (2) women assumed the role of judge; (3) Ruth and Naomi assumed roles different from those their culture prescribed; (4) the Song of Solomon celebrates the goodness of the sensual desire of a man and a woman for each other and presents the woman taking the initiative and being active in expressing her love (Doc. 8, p. 8). See also Ex. 1:15; 2:10; 15:20–21; Ruth 1—4; Judges 4—5; Song of Sol. 1—8.

What Was Jesus' Treatment of Women?

Jesus treated women as worthy human beings. Women were prominent among his followers. He freed women to assume roles and identities other than those the tradition prescribed (Doc. 8, p. 8). See also Mark 10:2–12; Luke 10:38–42; Matt. 5:27–28, 31–32.

How Did Paul Address This Issue?

Paul said that being baptized into Christ means that sexual distinctions are no longer important. This belief resulted in women's having significant places in leadership in local churches. In other passages, Paul's understanding of women shows much less belief in equality, but reflects the beliefs of the male-dominated culture of which he was a part (Doc. 8, p. 9). See also Gal. 3:23–29; 1 Cor. 11:2–16; 14:34–36.

What Does Our Church Say about Equality?

In sovereign love, God created the world good and makes everyone equally in God's image, male and female, of every race and people, to live as one community (Doc. 12, lines 29–32). See also Gen. 1:1—2:25; 5:1–32.

What Does Our Church Say about Equality in Church Life?

We affirm in the strongest possible terms that the body of Christ is made up of women and men. God calls both women and men to ministries in the life of the church. Any attempt to silence or marginalize any voices is not worthy of Christ's body (Doc. 13, p. 90).

Marriage

What Is Marriage?

A marriage is a covenant between a man and a woman in which they commit to live out their lives with each other. It is also an agreement that is licensed and regulated by the state (Doc. 7, pp. 7, 9, 12). See also Gen. 2:24–25.

What Is Christian Marriage?

A marriage is a Christian marriage when a couple make their covenant in the midst of a Christian community and when they acknowledge God's presence in their lives as they live out their relationship with each other. In a Christian marriage, a wife and husband promise to love and serve each other faithfully. God gives them the gift of sexual union as the sign of their mutual and lasting promise, as well as a means whereby they may share in creating new life (Doc. 7, pp. 9, 12; Doc. 4, lines 96–102). See also Mark 10:7–12; Gen. 2:24–25.

What Is God's Role in Marriage?

God established marriage. God preserves and guides all the relationships of life, and in marriage God works to increase love and faithfulness (Doc. 7, p. 9). See also Gen. 2:18–24.

Is It Necessary to Have a Wedding Ceremony to Have a Marriage?

A wedding ceremony is not necessary. Yet open acknowledgment of the covenant in the midst of the Christian community and seeking God's participation are needed. Some service akin to the wedding should be used (Doc. 7, p. 13).

How Should Married Couples Live?

A husband and wife are to love and care for each other in a relationship of equality (Doc. 7, p. 13). See also Mark 10:7–12; Eph. 5:21–23.

Procreation and Contraception

What Is the Purpose of Sexual Intercourse?

The primary purpose of sexual intercourse is to express love and intimate commitment. There does not need to be the intention to have children (Doc. 7, p. 14). See also Gen. 2:18–25.

Can a Marriage Be Fulfilled without Children?

A couple must decide this for themselves. It is quite possible that a couple might understand themselves and their gifts from God in such a way that their marriage could be fulfilled without children.

If married partners decide to become parents, their care for their children is intended to reflect God's love and discipline (Doc. 7, p. 14; Doc. 4, pp. 103–105).

What Does Our Church Believe about Contraception?

We believe any person who is physically capable of reproduction should have complete knowledge about contraceptives. We favor the general availability of contraceptive devices to persons who desire them. We consciously include the availability of contraceptives to unmarried persons in this recommendation (Doc. 3, p. 21; Doc. 10, p. 60).

Infertility

Does Our Church Support the Use of Medical Intervention in Cases of Infertility?

We affirm the use of drug and surgical therapies for problems that cause infertility (Doc. 9, p. 26).

Does Our Church Support Artificial Insemination?

We affirm the use of artificial insemination, with the husband as donor, as a responsible means of overcoming certain fertility problems (Doc. 9, p. 26).

Does Our Church Support Artificial Insemination by Donors other than the Husband?

We urge further study on the psychological, ethical, and legal ramifications for all parties, including the child, of using anonymous artificial insemination donors (Doc. 9, p. 26).

Does Our Church Support In Vitro Fertilization?

We affirm in vitro fertilization as a responsible alternative for couples for whom there is no other way to bear children, and oppose state or local legislation that would prohibit in vitro fertilization (Doc. 9, p. 26).

What Is Our Church's Position on Surrogate Motherhood?

We urge further study on the psychological, ethical, and legal ramifications for all parties, including the child (Doc. 9, p. 26).

Premarital Sex

What Is Premarital Sex?

Premarital sex means different things to different people. It can mean sexual intercourse that occurs as the result of a deliberate, thought-out act or just a spur-of-the-moment action. It could happen with an acquaintance, a friend, or a fiancée. It might occur during the course of a long-term relationship or on a casual date (Doc. 8, p. 16).

Should Teenagers Have Sexual Intercourse Before Marriage?

We believe it is best to postpone intercourse until marriage. If a teenage couple decides to have a sexual relationship, they have the responsibility to use effective contraception (Doc. 10, p. 51; Doc. 8, p. 16). See also Gen. 2:18–25.

What Does Our Church Believe about Premarital Sex?

We believe that total intimacy should happen in a relationship of total commitment, which marriage is intended to be. We advocate responsible behavior, understood as sexual expression that matches the seriousness and permanence of the relationship (Doc. 3, p. 29; Doc. 8, p. 16). See also Gen. 2:18–25.

If We Teach Young People about Contraception, Doesn't This Really Give Young People Permission to Engage in Sexual Intercourse?

No, young people should postpone sexual activity until marriage. Yet, in light of the number of teenage pregnancies that do occur, we would be failing in our ministry if we did not offer young people good contraceptive information (Doc. 10, p. 51).

Does Giving Young People Information about Contraception Lead to Greater Sexual Activity?

The most recent research shows that presentation of information about contraception serves both to delay the onset of sexual activity and to reduce its frequency (Doc. 10, p. 51).

What Options Does Our Church Offer a Pregnant Teenager Who Is Not Married?

The church offers the options of (1) marriage; (2) offering the child for adoption; (3) single parenthood; and (4) abortion (Doc. 10, pp. 50–51).

Extramarital Sex

What Is Extramarital Sex?

Extramarital sex is sexual intimacy with someone other than one's spouse. It is usually called adultery (Doc. 8, p. 17). See also Ex. 20:14.

What Does Jesus Teach about Extramarital Sex?

Jesus' teaching goes beyond the act to the state of the heart. Motivation and intent are the deciding factors. Evil that proceeds from the heart—whether it be adultery, greed, envy, arrogance, or malice—defiles people (Doc. 8, p. 8). See also Matt. 5:27–28; 7:20–23.

What Is Our Church's Teaching about Extramarital Sex?

Marriage is an unconditional covenant to be faithful to each other. Sexual intercourse outside such love and commitment to lifelong fidelity is not in keeping with the biblical understanding of God's intention for humanity (Doc. 8, pp. 9, 17; Doc. 7, p. 12; Doc. 4, lines 89–95). See also Ex. 20:14.

Should Married Couples Restrict Their Relationships with Others?

We were created to be in relation with other people. A marriage relationship should not limit other relationships, except that sexual activity is reserved for the intimacy of marriage (Doc. 7, p. 12). See also Ex. 20:14.

Sexual Abstinence

What Is Sexual Abstinence or Celibacy?

These terms mean refraining from sexual activity (Doc. 7, p 10).

Does Our Church Advocate Celibacy?

We believe celibacy is not good in itself, any more than is sexual activity. It can be a good choice for some Christian people if, like any sexual choice, it is life-affirming, other-affirming, and joyous— not life-rejecting, self-enclosed, and desolate (Doc. 8, p. 15). See also Gal. 5:22–23.

Does Our Church Believe That It Is Better to Be Single or to Be Married?

God wills both marriage and singleness. Each is God's gift and gifts may differ (Doc. 7, p. 10). See also 1 Cor. 12.

Masturbation

Why Would Someone Masturbate?

People masturbate for many reasons: curiosity about how it feels, as a way of releasing tension, as a release that afterward keeps them from thinking about sex so much, as a substitute for sexual relations when they do not have a spouse, or just because it feels good to them (Doc. 8, p. 15).

Is Masturbation a Good or a Bad Thing to Do?

Masturbation can be good or bad, depending on the reason someone decides to masturbate (Doc. 8, p. 15).

What Would Be Bad about Masturbation?

It could be a way of focusing on yourself rather than on relationships with other people. It could be a way of constantly satisfying yourself rather than seeing sexuality as a way of satisfying someone else. It could be done out of fear of becoming involved with someone else (Doc. 8, p. 15).

What Would Be Good about Masturbation?

Because masturbation lessens the sexual drive, it can make a sexual relationship with someone else a freer choice rather than something to which one is driven by sexual urges. It can be a good choice for those who are not married. It can be a good choice for those who cannot have sexual relations with a spouse because of absence, disability, or illness (Doc. 8, p. 15).

What Does Our Church Believe about Masturbation?

Masturbation is a normal part of growing up. There should be no guilt or shame for engaging in masturbation. Although we believe our sexuality is to be shared with someone else, masturbation can be a good choice to make in some circumstances (Doc. 8, p. 15; Doc. 3, pp. 14, 15).

Divorce

What Was Jesus' Attitude toward Divorce?

Jesus saw marriage as a permanent, lifelong, intimate personal union. Jesus himself, however, recognized that there are things that break marriage apart. He therefore acknowledged divorce as a reality, but without approving it (Doc. 7, p. 11). See also Mark 10:7–12.

What Is Our Church's Attitude toward Divorce?

We seek first reconciliation and the healing of brokenness in the marriage. Divorce is seen as legitimate, on the grounds of adultery or desertion, or where a continuation of the legal union would endanger the physical, moral, or spiritual well-being of one or both of the partners or that of their children (Doc. 7, p. 11).

Can Ministers and Officers of the Church Be Divorced?

Yes, officers and ministers whose marriages end in divorce may continue in their ministerial office. They should be counseled, helped, and forgiven just like everyone else in our community (Doc. 7, p. 12).

Abortion

Can the Choice of Abortion Be a Responsible Christian Choice?

In the exceptional case in which a woman is pregnant and judges that it would be irresponsible to bring a child into the world, given the limitations of her situation, it can be an act of faithfulness before God to intervene in the natural process of pregnancy and terminate it. Abortion may be considered a responsible and morally acceptable choice within the Christian faith when serious genetic problems arise or when the resources are not adequate to care for a child appropriately (Doc. 10, p. 58; Doc. 9, p. 10; Doc. 10, p. 32; Doc. 14, pp. 367–368).

What Is Our Primary Guide in Decision Making?

We can trust in God's Spirit to guide us in our decisions. We are part of the community of faith, and we can be sure that the community will be here to help and sustain us in our decisions. Furthermore, the gospel reminds us again and again of God's grace, which brings us love, care, and forgiveness (Doc. 10, p. 58). See also Rom. 8.

Who Has the Responsibility for Deciding about Abortion?

Biblical faith emphasizes the need for personal moral choice. Each individual is ultimately accountable to God for individual moral choices. The choice for an abortion is to be made by the woman who is in the position to make the decision, and it is, above all, her responsibility (Doc. 10, pp. 58, 60; Doc. 14, pp. 367–368).

When Should a Decision about Abortion Be Made?

A decision about abortion should be made as early as possible, generally within the first three months of the pregnancy. Abortions in the second three months are an option for those who do not discover they are pregnant until then, or for those who discover grave genetic disorders, or for those who have not had access to medical care during the first three months (Doc. 10, p. 59).

Should Abortion Be Available to Anyone Who Chooses It?

Our church believes we have a responsibility to guarantee every woman the freedom to choose for herself. Abortion should be made available to all who desire and qualify for it, not just to those who can afford it (Doc. 10, p. 60; Doc. 14, pp. 367–68).

Should a Woman Feel Guilty for Considering an Abortion?

A woman who considers abortion and then decides to continue her pregnancy should never be made to feel guilty that she has thought about abortion. It is far better to give birth intentionally than to feel that the diagnosis of pregnancy constitutes an absolute obligation to bear a child. In most pregnancies, the question of abortion will never arise, but when it does, the choice of abortion can be an expression of responsibility before God (Doc. 9, p. 10; Doc. 10, p. 32).

Should Abortion Be Considered a Form of Birth Control?

Abortion is not and should not be used as a form of birth control. It should not be chosen as a convenience or to ease embarrassment. It is a very serious and far-reaching decision (Doc. 11, p. 80; Doc. 14, pp. 367–368).

What Does Our Church Believe the Public Policy on Abortion Should Be?

We believe in Christian freedom and responsibility so that individuals can make their own choices, rather than have the state make decisions for them. We believe in a public policy of elective abortion, regulated by the health code, not the criminal code (Doc. 10, p. 52; Doc. 14, pp. 367–368).

What Does Our Church Believe about Violence at Women's Health Clinics?

Our church condemns violence and threats of violence at women's health clinics, and encourages individuals to use language and images responsibly to avoid stimulating or encouraging violence or appearing to condone violent behavior (Doc. 15, pp. 678–679).

Are There Varieties of Beliefs about Abortion Within Our Church?

Yes, there is a great variety of beliefs, and those who hold these varying beliefs tend to hold them very strongly. It is for this reason that our church has been led to the conviction that the decision regarding abortion must remain with the individual, to be made on the basis of conscience and personal religious principles (Doc. 10, p. 60).

Homosexuality

Who Is Considered Homosexual?

Anyone who experiences repeated, intense attraction to a person or persons of the same sex is considered to be homosexual. Such a definition excludes the casual experimenter (Doc. 5, p. 971).

Are People Either Homosexual or Heterosexual?

It is believed that most people exist somewhere on a continuum that ranges from an exclusively heterosexual orientation to one that is exclusively homosexual (Doc. 5, p. 971).

Are People Created as Either Male or Female?

God created us male and female, but the process of creation is not finished, either chemically or psychologically, at birth. Our development process continues through adolescence, at the end of which we establish a comfortable identity with our given sexuality (Doc. 3, p. 17; Doc. 5, p. 972).

What Is Meant by "Gay" and "Lesbian"?

As used by the homosexual community, the words *gay* and *lesbian* are adjectives or nouns that refer to homosexual orientation, respectively, in a man and in a woman. Originally used by heterosexual persons as derogatory labels for homosexual persons, the terms have now been claimed by many homosexual persons as words that describe the full joy of their self-acceptance as homosexuals (Doc. 5, p. 977).

How Does Someone Become Heterosexual or Homosexual?

No one can say for sure why some people are heterosexual and some are homosexual. The majority of human beings develop a heterosexual orientation. Some people believe that homosexuality is determined biologically, while others believe that societal forces play a large role (Doc. 5, p. 972–974).

Do Gays and Lesbians Choose to Be Homosexual?

Most gay and lesbian adults have no awareness of having "chosen" homosexuality. In early adolescence, when fantasies of others focused on the opposite sex, theirs focused on the same sex. In later adolescence, when others enjoyed dating, they did not. In early adulthood, when others fell in and out of love with the opposite sex, they fell in and out of love with the same sex. Somehow, in some inexplicable way, something "different" had happened to them. Without knowing how or why, they believe they were created as homosexual (Doc. 5, p. 974).

What Is Homophobia?

Homophobia is contempt, hatred, or fear of people who are gay or lesbian (Doc. 5, p. 1021).

How Does Our Church View Homophobia?

We believe there can be no place within the Christian faith for homophobia. Persons who manifest homosexual behavior must be treated with the profound respect and pastoral tenderness due all people of God (Doc. 5, p. 1021).

Does Our Church Believe Gays and Lesbians Should Be Welcome in the Church?

We believe gay and lesbian persons are loved by Christ. We believe the church must turn from its fear and hatred to move toward the gay and lesbian community in love and to welcome gay and lesbian inquirers into our congregations (Doc. 5, p. 1021).

Do Gays and Lesbians Need to Change or Hide Their Behavior in Order to Become a Part of the Church?

We believe gays and lesbians should be free to be candid about their identity and convictions. There is room in the church for all who give honest affirmation to the vows required for membership in the church. Gay and lesbian persons who sincerely affirm, "Jesus Christ is my Lord and Savior" and "I intend to be his disciple, to obey his word, and to show his love" should not be excluded from membership (Doc. 5, p. 1021).

Can a Gay or Lesbian Person Be Ordained as an Officer or Minister in the Church?

Our church's present understanding is that persons who do not repent of homosexual practice cannot be officers or ministers (Doc. 5, p. 1022).

Can a Gay or Lesbian Person Who Does Not Act Out His/Her Homosexuality Be Ordained?

The repentant gay or lesbian person who finds the power of Christ redirecting his or her sexual desires toward a married heterosexual commitment, or who finds God's power to control his or her desires and to adopt a celibate lifestyle, can certainly be ordained, all other qualifications being met. Indeed, such candidates must be welcomed and made free to share their full identity (Doc. 5, p. 1022).

Can Any Committee of the Church Ask What a Person's Sexual Orientation Is?

No, it is up to the individual to take the initiative in declaring his or her sexual orientation (Doc. 5, p. 1022).

What Is Our Church's Understanding of Laws That Discriminate Against a Person on the Basis of Sexual Orientation?

We believe we should work to oppose laws that discriminate against persons on the basis of sexual orientation. In addition, we should initiate and support laws that prohibit discrimination against persons on the basis of sexual orientation (Doc. 5, pp. 1005, 1023; Doc. 16, pp. 118–119).

Is There Disagreement with This Understanding of Homosexuality within Our Church?

Yes, there are those within the church who believe that gays and lesbians should be ordained as officers and ministers. There are also those who believe that homosexuality is sinful. The stand of our church is to encourage all church members to continue dialogue within the church. We believe there is always the possibility for more light to break forth from God's Spirit to aid our understanding (Doc. 5, pp. 978, 1024).

Sexual Misconduct

What Is Our Church's Position on Sexual Misconduct?

Sexual misconduct is a misuse of authority and power that breaches Christian ethical principles by misusing a trust relationship to gain advantage over another for personal pleasure in an abusive, exploitive, and unjust manner. Sexual misconduct takes advantage of the vulnerability of children and persons who are less powerful to act for their own welfare. It violates the mandate to protect the vulnerable from harm (Doc. 17, pp. 76–92).

Decision Making

What Is Our Authority in Deciding Issues About Human Sexuality?

The Bible is our authority, as it is understood and interpreted within the church (Doc. 8, p. 7).

Does the Bible Have an Answer for Every Question about Sexuality?

The Bible primarily tells about God, God's community, and God's grace toward us. The Bible is not a catalog of infallible prescriptions concerning each moral problem we face (Doc. 8, p. 7).

Do People in Our Church Live Out Their Sexuality in the Way God Intended?

Like all people, we act from mixed motives and divided intentions. All of us fail in some ways (Doc. 8, p. 12).

Do All Members of Our Church Agree on How to Live Out Our Sexuality?

No, a variety of opinions exist on what constitutes responsible sexuality. Christians may behave in good conscience in ways that other conscientious Christians, in good conscience, neither approve of nor understand (Doc. 8, p. 12).

What, Then, Is the Role of Our Church in Human Sexuality?

Our church is a place where people experience forgiveness and help in living out their sexuality, rather than rejection and condemnation because they have fallen short of God's intention and their own best aspirations. The church is a community of forgiven sinners. When we fail each other as parents or partners, we are called to forgive each other as God forgives us and to accept the possibilities for renewal that God offers us in grace (Doc. 8, p. 12; Doc. 4, lines 106–109). See also Rom. 3:21–26; 8.

Find Someone Who . . .

Directions: Find different people in your group who match these statements and ask them to sign their names beside that statement. Do not sign your own name.

Find someone who . . .

1. has not been to a movie in the last month. _____

2. walks to school. _____

3. has three sisters. _____

4. is going to high school next year. _____

5. is allergic to chocolate. _____

6. dislikes pizza. _____

7. is over 5' 6" tall. _____

8. you have never met before. _____

9. you have met before. _____

10. cannot rollerblade. _____

11. gets Bs or better in math. _____

12. is left handed. _____

13. has never been on water skis. _____

14. prefers yellow as a favorite color. _____

15. knows how to play hockey. _____

16. is an only child. _____

17. has a part-time job. _____

18. prefers hamburgers to pizza. _____

Anatomy Drawing (Male)

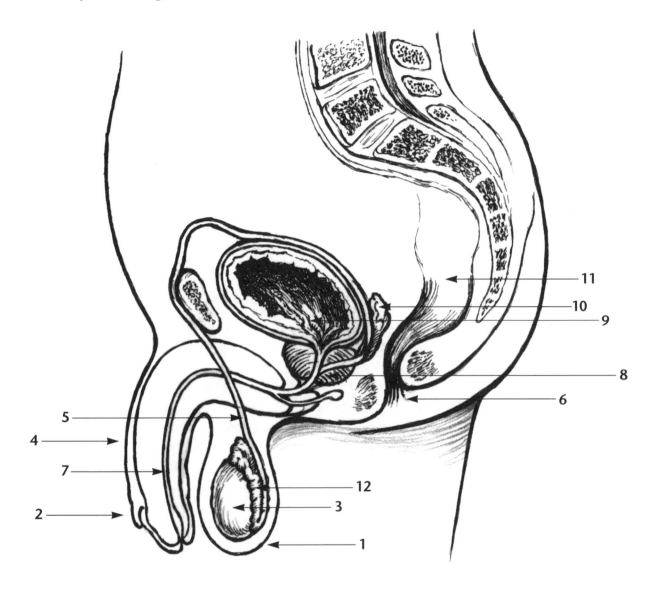

Scrotum	Penis	Anus
Vas deferens	Prostate gland	Glans penis
Testis	Urethra	Epididymis
Bladder	Rectum	Seminal vesicle

1. _____
2. _____
3. _____
4. _____
5. _____
6. _____

7. _____
8. _____
9. _____
10. _____
11. _____
12. _____

Anatomy Drawing (Female—Internal)

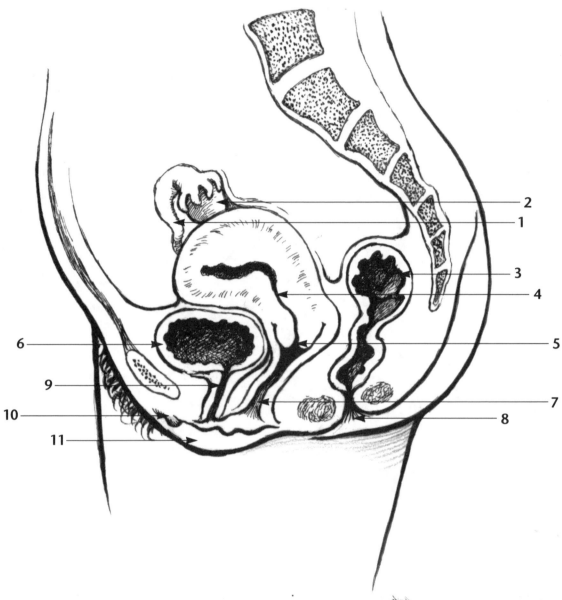

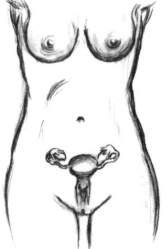

Urethra	Vagina	Anus
Bladder	Fallopian tube	Rectum
Labia	Uterus (womb)	Clitoris
Cervix	Ovary	

1. _____
2. _____
3. _____
4. _____
5. _____
6. _____

7. _____
8. _____
9. _____
10. _____
11. _____

Anatomy Drawing (Female—External)

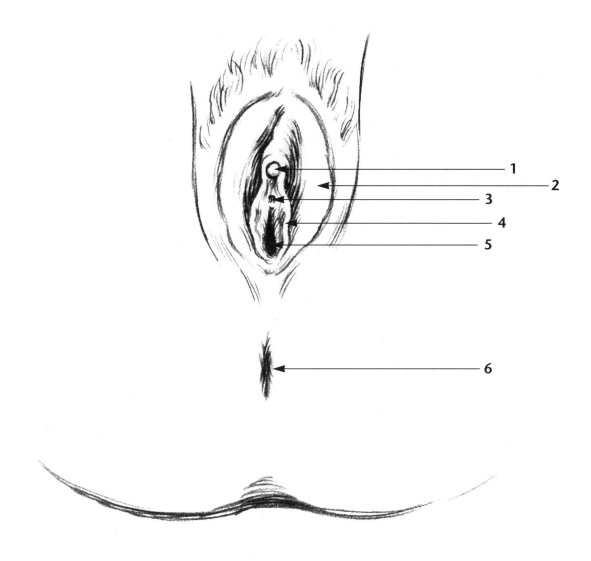

Labia minora (inner lips)   Anus (opening)   Labia majora (outer lips)
Urethra (opening)   Clitoris   Vagina (opening)

1. _____   4. _____
2. _____   5. _____
3. _____   6. _____

Anatomy Drawings—Answer Key

Male

1. Scrotum
2. Glans penis
3. Testis
4. Penis
5. Vas deferens
6. Anus
7. Urethra
8. Prostate gland
9. Bladder
10. Seminal vesicle
11. Rectum
12. Epididymis

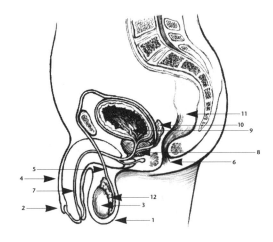

Female (Internal)

1. Fallopian tube
2. Ovary
3. Rectum
4. Uterus (womb)
5. Cervix
6. Bladder
7. Vagina
8. Anus
9. Urethra
10. Clitoris
11. Labia

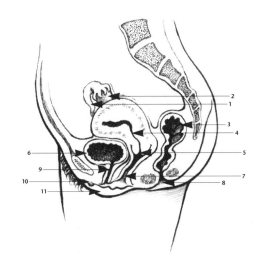

Female (External)

1. Clitoris
2. Labia majora (outer lips)
3. Urethra (opening)
4. Labia minora (inner lips)
5. Vagina (opening)
6. Anus (opening)

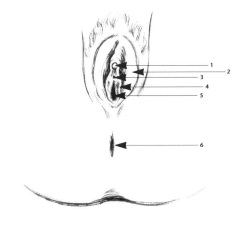

Male Physiology Sheet

A. Semen
B. Circumcision
C. Glans
D. Erection
E. Epididymis

F. Impotence
G. Penis
H. Ejaculation
I. Scrotum
J. Foreskin

K. Vas deferens
L. Testes
M. Sperm
N. Premature ejaculation
O. Seminal vesicles

1. _____ The stiffening of the penis because of an increased flow of blood.

2. _____ Male sex cells that fertilize the ovum or egg.

3. _____ The sack of skin that forms a pouch containing the testicles.

4. _____ Tube through which the sperm travel from testicles to the seminal vesicles and urethra.

5. _____ Male sex organ used in urination and intercourse.

6. _____ Whitish fluid in which sperm is transported and ejaculated.

7. _____ The inability to achieve an erection.

8. _____ Covering of the tip of the penis that is often removed.

9. _____ A vast group of microscopic tubes where sperm are stored.

10. _____ Orgasm and discharge of semen before the penis has completely entered the vagina or just after entry.

11. _____ The tip of the penis.

12. _____ Surgical removal of the foreskin of the penis, which covers the glans.

13. _____ Male sex glands.

14. _____ Pouches that open out into the sperm ducts.

15. _____ The rapid discharge or expulsion of sperm and semen during orgasm.

Female Physiology Sheet

A. Abortion
B. Fallopian tube
C. Ovary
D. Vulva
E. Cervix

F. Hymen
G. Ovulation
H. Vagina
I. Clitoris
J. Labia

K. Placenta
L. Ovum
M. Douche
N. Menarche
O. Uterus

1. _____ The name of the female sex cell, derived from the Latin word for egg.

2. _____ A process used mistakenly as a contraceptive and sometimes to cleanse the vagina.

3. _____ The place where the egg is fertilized.

4. _____ A center of sexual response for women.

5. _____ The start of menstruation.

6. _____ The approximate monthly release of an ovum.

7. _____ The removal of a fetus from the uterus prior to birth, sometimes occurring spontaneously.

8. _____ The lips or folds of skin covering the vaginal opening. There are two sets: majora and minora.

9. _____ The term that applies to both sets of the structures referred to in number 8.

10. _____ The twin storage places for ova (eggs) in the female.

11. _____ A thin membrane across the opening of the vagina.

12. _____ A pear-shaped organ where the fertilized ovum develops into a fetus.

13. _____ The opening, sometimes called the birth canal, where the penis enters during intercourse.

14. _____ The neck of the uterus where the vagina and uterus are joined.

15. _____ The lining of the uterus through which the baby is fed during pregnancy.

Male and Female Physiology Sheets—Answer Key

Male Physiology	*Female Physiology*
1. D	1. L
2. M	2. M
3. I	3. B
4. K	4. I
5. G	5. N
6. A	6. G
7. F	7. A
8. J	8. J
9. E	9. D
10. N	10. C
11. C	11. F
12. B	12. O
13. L	13. H
14. O	14. E
15. H	15. K

God Created Us and Gave Us the Gift of Our Sexuality

> Then God said, "Let us make humankind in our image, according to our likeness; and let them have dominion over . . . the earth." So God created humankind in [God's] image, in the image of God [God] created them; male and female [God] created them . . . God saw everything that God had made, and indeed, it was very good.
>
> (Gen. 1:26, 27, 31a)

> For we are what [God] has made us, created in Christ Jesus for good works.
>
> (Eph. 2:10)

God created us and called us very good. God did not create us only as spirits, nor only as bodies. God created us as total persons—body and spirit. And God called this entire creation very good.

Not only did God create us, but God created us to be God's very own image in the world. All that we are—including our bodies, including our sexuality—is God's gift to us.

Our sexuality is our way of being male or female in the world. Our sexuality is very basic; it affects our thoughts, feelings, and actions. Because our sexuality is called good by God and because it is God's gift to us, we can feel good about our sexuality.

Questions

1. The first point in understanding our sexuality is to understand that it is God's good gift to us. What is good for you about being male or female?

_____

_____

_____

_____

2. Do you think most people your age believe sexuality is a positive part of their lives? If not, how do they feel about their sexuality?

_____

_____

_____

_____

3. What is difficult about being female or male?

_____

_____

_____

_____

4. What do you not understand about being a male?

_____

_____

_____

_____

5. What do you not understand about being a female?

_____

_____

_____

6. Do you think it is easier for males or for females to feel good about their sexuality? Why?

_____

_____

_____

_____

7. Do you think your parents feel good about your sexual development? Do they talk to you about your sexual development?

_____

_____

_____

_____

8. Your body may be going through many changes. What changes would you describe as embarrassing, as difficult, or as very good?

_____

_____

_____

_____

9. Your body is still in the process of changing. What changes do you still want to see happen?

_____

_____

_____

_____

10. In one word, God described your sexuality as "good." What one word would you use?

_____

_____

_____

_____

Litany

Leader: In the book of Genesis, God said: "Let's make humankind in our own image . . . " So God created humankind in God's own image, in the image of God was the human being created; male and female God created them.

All: God created us together—to be together. That is what Scripture says. God made us male and female, boys and girls, men and women. That is all part of God's plan for the enjoyment and fulfillment of human life.

Girls: To be a growing female is hard. I like being a girl, but it is hard to understand and to know what life holds for me. I feel so mixed up at times. I want to laugh and cry at the same time. I want to feel like a woman. I am glad God created me female. Thank you, God!

Boys: To be a growing male is hard. I like being a boy, but it is hard to understand and to know what life holds for me. At times I feel all mixed up inside, like I should hide. I want to feel like a man. I am glad God created me male. Thank you, God!

All: Creator of us all, we need you as our friend and guide as we grow to be men and women. Teach us the way of love as we spend time together, as we talk, play, and live together. Teach us the meaning of love as we learn and grow, as we date and form relationships with one another.

Teach us the depths of love as we learn to give of ourselves to others.

Creator of goodness and beauty, you tell us that love is beautiful and good. Let our activities together express your love. Let us treat our bodies as holy temples. Let us care for each other as you care for us. Amen.

Love, Infatuation, and Friendship Definitions

Love . . .

is a slowly developing and exciting experience.

is energizing.

lets people enjoy everything in life.

occurs between two people who feel good about themselves.

rarely involves jealousy or possessiveness.

comes from two people honestly sharing their feelings.

involves a commitment over time and through difficulty.

Love . . .

is patient and kind.

is not jealous or conceited or proud.

is not ill-mannered or selfish or irritable.

does not keep a record of wrongs.

is not happy with evil.

is happy with the truth.

never gives up.

is faith, hope, and patience that never fails.

is eternal.

(paraphrased from 1 Cor. 13)

Infatuation . . .

is a quickly developing experience.

is exhausting—people can think of nothing else.

keeps people from focusing on other parts of life.

is sometimes motivated by a desire to be taken care of.

occurs when someone feels that he or she is a nobody who can become somebody with the other person.

is often jealous and possessive.

comes from two people denying their conflicting feelings.

does not last over time or through difficulty.

Friendship . . .

occurs with communication.

occurs among people who share common interests.

involves listening.

may turn into love.

occurs with acceptance and trust.

occurs between two people who enjoy each other.

can last over time and through difficulty.

Love, Infatuation, and Friendship Situations

Jill and Eric both play the clarinet in band. They have known each other for three years and often practice together. Wednesday, Eric asked Jill to go to the basketball game.

Martin met Shawna while on vacation at the beach last year. They spent lots of time together during the week and had a great time. Martin knew Shawna was special. He knew he was in love. This fall they have written each other several times, but now the letters are coming less frequently.

Sam and Soon Lee have been looking at (but pretending not to notice) each other for several weeks now. Finally, Sam called Soon Lee and asked her to go steady. She said yes. After hanging up, she called her friend Julie and told her she was in love.

Rose and Jim have lived down the street from each other for years. About twice a month they go for a bicycle ride. Lately when they reach the park, they stop and talk about school, parents, and friends.

Marcus and Cindy have been going steady for one year. They occasionally have "real" dates, but often they spend time together doing things with their families. What Cindy and Marcus like most about their relationship is the way they can talk to each other. Once in a while they have an argument, but they keep talking until things are worked out.

Juan and Jeff are inseparable. They go to the movies together, are on the same football team, spend the night at each other's houses, and often study with each other.

Ann and Joon have been going together for fourteen weeks. Lately Ann has become angry at Joon when he talks to other girls.

Homosexuality Quiz

Directions: Answer each statement True (T), False (F), or do not know (DK).

1. _____ Homosexuality is feeling attracted to or turned on mostly by members of one's own sex.

2. _____ We know homosexuality is caused by an imbalance of hormones.

3. _____ Homosexuals are born that way.

4. _____ More males than females are homosexual.

5. _____ You can easily tell homosexuals by the way they dress or act.

6. _____ Most homosexuals are child molesters.

7. _____ Once a person has a homosexual experience, then he or she is a homosexual.

8. _____ Most churches see homosexual behavior as sinful.

9. _____ About one-third of all males engage in homosexual behavior at some point in their lives.

10. _____ Almost all people have homosexual feelings at one time or another, but they usually won't admit it.

11. _____ Women who are successful in their careers are often lesbians (a term for female homosexuals).

12. _____ Homosexuals are more creative than heterosexuals.

13. _____ A male can do things traditionally considered feminine and not be a homosexual.

14. _____ A female can do things traditionally considered masculine and not be a homosexual.

Homosexuality Quiz—Answer Key

1. Homosexuality is feeling attracted to or turned on mostly by members of one's own sex. **True.**

2. We know homosexuality is caused by an imbalance of hormones. **False.**

3. Homosexuals are born that way. **Do not know.**

4. More males than females are homosexual. **True.**

5. You can easily tell homosexuals by the way they dress or act. **False.**

6. Most homosexuals are child molesters. **False.**

7. Once a person has a homosexual experience, then he or she is a homosexual. **False.**

8. Most churches see homosexual behavior as sinful. **True.**

9. About one-third of all males engage in homosexual behavior at some point in their lives. **True.**

10. Almost all people have homosexual feelings at one time or another, but they usually won't admit it. **True.**

11. Women who are successful in their careers are often lesbians (a term for female homosexuals). **False.**

12. Homosexuals are more creative than heterosexuals. **False.**

13. A male can do things traditionally considered feminine and not be a homosexual. **True.**

14. A female can do things traditionally considered masculine and not be a homosexual. **True.**

Beliefs about Homosexuality

1. What is homosexuality?

2. What do people believe the causes of homosexuality may be?

3. What does our church say about the relationship between membership in the church and being homosexual?

4. What is homophobia?

5. What additional information would help you better understand homosexuality?

6. How would you express your feelings about those who are homosexual?

Definitions

Usually, people are attracted to someone of the opposite gender—males to females, and females to males. We don't know why. It's the way God created them. It's just a part of who they are deep inside. A word used to describe people who are sexually attracted to people of the opposite gender is *heterosexual.*

Some people are sexually attracted to people of the same gender—males to males, and females to females. We don't know why. Most of the people who are this way think it's because God created them this way. A word used to describe people who are sexually attracted to people of the same gender is *homosexual.*

Sexually Transmitted Infections (STIs)

Acquired Immune Deficiency Syndrome (AIDS)

What is it?

AIDS, caused by HIV, a virus that destroys the body's immune system allowing life-threatening illnesses to attack the body.

How do I get it?

By the transfer of infected body fluids through sex, sharing dirty needles, or from contaminated blood.

Is it common?

It continues to spread.

How do I get rid of it?

There is no cure, but new medications are being developed to help control it.

Chlamydia

What is it?

Bacterial infection in the urinary and reproductive organs.

How do I get it?

Close sexual contact with someone infected, even without intercourse.

Is it common?

It is the most common STI in the United States, with four million new cases each year.

How do I get rid of it?

The right antibiotic.

Gonorrhea

What is it?

Bacterial infection inside the body.

How do I get it?

Close sexual contact with someone infected, even without intercourse.

Is it common?

There are one million new cases each year.

How do I get rid of it?

The right antibiotic.

Hepatitis B

What is it?

Viral infection causing inflammation of the liver.

How do I get it?

Exposure to infected blood or body fluids or dirty needles.

Is it common?

Very common.

How do I get rid of it?

Bed rest for several weeks, maybe months.

Herpes

What is it?

Painful blisters on the penis, vagina, or anus.

How do I get it?

The virus enters the body through cuts or sexual contact.

Is it common?

There are five hundred thousand to one million new cases each year.

How do I get rid of it?

No cure, only medical relief of pain.

Human Papilloma Virus (HPV)

What is it?

HPV, also known as genital warts, a viral infection that causes warts.

How do I get it?

The virus enters the body through sexual contact or use of damp linens or bathing suits that have been used by someone infected.

Is it common?

It is spreading rapidly among teenagers.

How do I get rid of it?

The warts are treated with ointment, frozen, or burned off with a laser or electric needle.

Scabies, Lice

What is it?

Lice are tiny crabs that live in the hair around the penis or vagina; scabies are tiny bugs that burrow under the skin.

How do I get it?

Sexual contact with someone infected, or by using a towel, toilet seat, bedding, or clothing used by someone infected.

Is it common?

Fairly common.

How do I get rid of it?

Creams, lotions, shampoos that clean the body.

Syphilis

What is it?

Bacterial infection.

How do I get it?

Sexual contact with sores from infected person to an open cut on another.

Is it common?

It is increasing among teenagers.

How do I get rid of it?

Penicillin or other antibiotic.

Trichomoniasis

What is it?

Infection of vagina in women, urethra in men, caused by tiny protozoa.

How do I get it?

Sexual contact with someone infected, or by using a towel, toilet seat, bedding, or clothing used by someone infected.

Is it common?

Very common.

How do I get rid of it?

A specific antibiotic.

Ten Most Commonly Asked Questions about STIs

1. Can I get AIDS if I'm not gay?

Yes. AIDS is a disease caused by a virus (HIV), so anyone exposed to the virus can get AIDS. AIDS is decreasing among gay people (education is encouraging them to employ healthy behaviors to avoid HIV), but it is increasing among the heterosexual population, especially young women.

2. Are STIs, other than AIDS, really a serious threat?

Yes. Many of them are life-threatening if not treated. Some are not life-threatening, but cannot be cured and can cause pain for a lifetime. Some can lead to the development of other illnesses, including cancer, and can cause pregnancy complications.

3. Are women at a greater risk for STIs?

Yes. It is often easier for a woman's body to catch and hold diseases, and often those infections are difficult to detect. Annual exams help women protect themselves.

4. Could I have an STI and not even know it?

Yes. Many people with STIs experience no noticeable symptoms. Regular check-ups help people discover disease.

5. Can condoms prevent STIs?

Maybe. Latex condoms, when used correctly, are effective in *reducing* the transmission of most infections. But condoms often are used incorrectly or only occasionally. No method except abstinence is 100 percent effective.

6. Can STIs be cured?

Some can, some can't. Bacterial STIs (including gonorrhea, chlamydia, and syphilis) can be cured with antibiotics. Viral STIs (including AIDS and herpes) cannot.

7. Can I test myself for STIs?

You can start the process. You might be able to recognize what could be symptoms of an STI. Or you could use a home HIV test. But laboratory tests are necessary to confirm an STI and to prescribe proper treatment.

8. Can I get AIDS from shaking hands with someone who has AIDS?

No. You cannot get AIDS from shaking hands, drinking from a water fountain, touching, hugging, or kissing. You also cannot get AIDS from toilet seats, swimming pools, public showers, sneezes, coughs, donating blood, or being around someone who has AIDS.

9. Can I get an STI from a towel or a toilet seat?

Yes. Lice, scabies, and trichomoniasis can be caught from infected towels, clothes, or sheets (and maybe in a rare instance from a toilet seat), but most STIs are spread only through direct sexual contact.

10. Is there such a thing as safer sex?

Yes. Safer sex means using a condom and being sure your partner has no STI. Safe sex happens if a couple has no STIs and is in a committed relationship where they have no other sexual partners.

Birth Control Chart

Method	How to Use It/Cost	Actual Rate of Effectiveness
Pill	Woman takes one pill a day, which prevents release of egg. ($25 to $45 for a month's supply)	97%
Implant	Woman has six small tubes implanted in her upper arm, which prevent release of egg. ($450 to $900 for implanting; lasts five years)	99.91%
Injection	Woman receives an injection, which prevents release of egg. ($30 to $65 for the injection, which lasts three months)	99.7%
IUD	A doctor places the IUD in the woman's uterus, which keeps eggs from implanting. ($250 to $750 for the device, which can last ten years)	99.2%
Diaphragm	A soft, rubber dome is placed far inside the vagina, over the cervix, which prevents sperm from entering the uterus. ($20 to $50 for the diaphragm)	82%
Condom	For a male, a latex sheath is placed over the penis, which prevents sperm from entering the woman. (Each condom costs 50 cents to $3.50 and can be used only once.) For a female, a latex sheath is placed to line the vagina and cover the cervix so sperm cannot enter the uterus. (Each condom costs $1.50 to $3.50 and can be used only once.)	Male condom, 88% Female condom, 79%
Abstinence	No sexual intercourse (no cost)	100%
Sterilization	For a female, the tubes are cut, which keeps the egg from entering the uterus. For a male, the tube carrying the sperm from the testes to the penis is cut so that the sperm cannot be ejaculated. (Costs vary greatly for the surgery, which is permanent.)	Male, 99.85% Female, 99.6%
Natural Family Planning	Woman does not have sexual intercourse during the times in her cycle when she is most likely to get pregnant. (Cost is for a thermometer and chart to keep track of the monthly cycle).	65% to 80%

Beliefs about Abortion

Listed below are some conflicting viewpoints about abortion. Pick the one that represents our church's belief. Tell why it is our belief. Tell whether you agree or disagree with it.

1.   A. Choosing to have an abortion might be the right choice for a Christian to make.

   B. Choosing to have an abortion would never be the right choice for a Christian to make.

   C. Choosing to have an abortion is always the right choice for a Christian to make.

Answer: A. Abortion might be the right choice in situations such as when serious genetic problems arise or when the resources are not adequate to care for a child.

2.   A. We can trust in God's Spirit, God's Word, and God's people to help us make the right decision about an abortion.

   B. God's Word tells us that abortion is always wrong.

   C. The church teaches us that humans do not have the ability to make life-and-death choices; only God does.

Answer: A. We can trust in God's Spirit to guide us in all our decisions; the gospel reminds us again and again of God's grace; we are part of the community of faith and we can be sure that the community will be there to help and sustain us in our decisions.

3.   A. The ultimate decision about an abortion is the responsibility of the doctor of the woman who is pregnant.

   B. The ultimate decision about an abortion is the responsibility of the woman who is pregnant.

   C. The ultimate decision about an abortion is the responsibility of the church.

Answer: B. Biblical faith emphasizes the need for personal moral choice, with each individual ultimately accountable to God. The choice for an abortion is to be made by the woman who is in the position to make the decision, and it is, above all, her responsibility.

4.   A. Abortion should be available to anyone who can pay for it.

   B. Abortion should be available for anyone who can show a reasonable reason for choosing it.

   C. Abortion should be available to anyone who chooses it.

Answer: C. We have responsibility to guarantee every woman the freedom to choose for herself.

5.   A. It is wrong for a woman to think about an abortion.

   B. It is wrong for a woman to think about an abortion, and then decide not to have one.

   C. It is okay for a woman to think about an abortion.

Answer: C. It is better to give birth intentionally than to feel that the diagnosis of pregnancy constitutes an absolute obligation to bear a child. A woman who considers abortion should never be made to feel guilty that she has thought about it.

6.   A. Abortion is often an easy and convenient choice for a woman who does not want to be pregnant.

   B. Abortion is a good way to ease the embarrassment some women might feel if they are pregnant.

   C. Abortion is not a form of birth control.

Answer: C. Abortion is a very serious and far-reaching decision, so it should not be considered as a form of birth control or chosen as a convenience or to ease embarrassment.

7.   A. Most people in our church believe abortion is morally wrong.

   B. Most people in our church believe abortion is morally acceptable.

   C. There are varieties of beliefs about abortion within our church.

Answer: C. There are many beliefs and a great variety of words that people in our church would use to describe their beliefs concerning abortion. Many of the varying beliefs are held very strongly by individuals. It is for this reason that the church has been led to the conviction that the decision regarding abortion must remain with the individual, to be made on the basis of conscience and personal religious principles.

Sexuality and Violence

Julie

When Julie was thirteen, she had her first date. Matt was also thirteen and one of the cutest guys in the eighth grade. Julie was really excited to go out with him. All of her friends had been talking about their boyfriends and now she had a date. On Friday night, he told her he was babysitting for his younger brother and asked her to come over to watch a movie. When she got there, Matt's younger brother was just going to bed. She and Matt hung out for a while and then they started the movie. During the movie, Matt sat really close to Julie, which felt good to her. But then he started kissing her too hard. When she said "no," Matt held her down and forced her to have sex with him.

André

When André was twelve, he was still pretty short and slim for his age. He went out for the football team, but he didn't ever start. He mostly warmed the bench. He also played in the orchestra and was really good. One day he bumped into Brad by mistake. Brad was really popular and was a starter on the football team. Brad got really mad and pushed him. From that day on, whenever Brad saw André, he would push him and tell him he was gay because he played the violin. In the locker room during gym class, Brad and his friends would make fun of André's body as he changed clothes.

What We Need to Know*

Males

Regarding Rape

- Understand that "no" means "no."
- Know that it is never okay to force yourself on a girl, even if you think she's been teasing you and leading you on, even if you've heard that women say "no" when they really mean "yes."
- Know that it is never okay to force yourself on a girl, even if you feel physically that you've got to have sex.
- Know that it is never okay to force yourself on a girl, even if she is drunk.
- Know that whenever you use force to have sex you are committing a crime

called rape even if you know her or have had sex with her before.
- Be aware of peer pressure to "score," and work against it by listening to what your date is saying.
- Be aware of what society may tell you it means to be a "real" man, and work against it by forming your own values based on respect, honesty, good listening skills, and so forth.
- Recognize that you can be raped too.

Regarding Harassment

- Be aware of what your peers may be telling you about being "cool"; avoid putting others down.
- Work on your own self-image, which is based on respect for other people, not on being better than someone else.

Females

Regarding Rape

- Say "no" when you mean "no"; say "yes" when you mean "yes"; stay in touch with your feelings to know the difference.
- Believe in your right to express your feelings and learn to do so assertively.
- Be aware of stereotypes that prevent you from expressing yourself, such as "anger is unfeminine," "being polite, pleasant, and quiet is feminine."
- Be aware of specific situations in which you do not feel relaxed and "in charge."
- Be aware of situations in which you are vulnerable and have fewer resources.
- Be aware that if you are raped, it is not your fault, you didn't deserve it, and you can get help.

Regarding Harassment

- Remember that you have the right to your feelings and your space.
- If you have experienced harassment, remember that you are not alone, you can report it and get help.

*Excerpted from *Sexual Abuse Prevention: A Course of Study for Teenagers*, by Rebecca Voelkel-Haugen and Marie Fortune (Cleveland: United Church Press, 1996), 22. Used by permission.

Self-Esteem Exercise

1. The good feelings of esteem come from a variety of places—from other people, from things you do, from special times and places. From what other sources might people receive reinforcement of their self-esteem? Add them to the list.

- your mother
- your father
- a grandparent
- a brother or a sister
- a teacher
- an adult at church
- God
- an accomplishment at school
- some special words of praise
- a good friend
- a celebration, such as a birthday or Christmas
- something you did for someone else
- a special skill you have
- a certain thing about your personality
- something brave you did
- a special place you like to be
- your own feelings about yourself
- _____
- _____
- _____

2. Circle the things above that are sources of esteem for you. Then beside each one you have circled, explain exactly how it is a source of esteem.
3. Self-esteem happens when we realize:

   We were created by God.
   God believes we are one of God's good creations.
   Others love and affirm us.
   All of us make mistakes but when we recognize and admit our mistakes, God is with us, forgiving us, no matter what we have done.

Amy and Joe*

Amy and Joe have been going together for three months. Joe leaves town with his parents for a long summer vacation. Amy and Joe have agreed not to date anyone else in the meantime.

David, a friend of Joe's, knows that Joe and Amy are going together, but he asks Amy out anyway. She doesn't know whether to accept or say no, so she asks the advice of her friend Jane. Jane says, "Just do what you think is best."

Amy decides to go out with David. They have several dates while Joe is on vacation. They stop dating when Joe returns.

Joe confesses to Amy that he dated a girl while he was on his vacation. Amy gets very angry with Joe and feels hurt. She tells him she never wants to see him again and that she no longer trusts him.

1. Who did you like best in the "Amy and Joe" story? Why?

2. Who did you like least in this story? Why?

3. Which of the three characters acted most responsibly? Why?

4. Which one acted most irresponsibly? Why?

5. Which of the following dating patterns do you think is best?

a.   To go out with one person exclusively.

b.   To go out with a lot of different people and be honest about it.

c.   To go out with whomever you want but not mention to any of your dates that you are also dating others.

6. Which of the following do you think is the worst thing to hear about a friend?

a.   The friend has an STI.

b.   The friend is "sleeping around" with a lot of people.

c.   The friend is telling lies about the people he or she is dating.

---

*Adapted from "My Feelings Are Me," in *Growing Up to Love*. Youth Elect Series (St. Louis: Christian Board of Publication), p. 31. Used with permission.

Our Church Is a Community of Love and Responsibility

> By contrast, the fruit of the Spirit is love, joy, peace, patience, kindness, generosity, faithfulness, gentleness, and self-control.
>
> (Gal. 5: 22–23a)

> God has told you . . . what is good; and what does the Lord require of you but to do justice, and to love kindness, and to walk humbly with your God?
>
> (Micah 6:8)

We are created to be in community, in relationship with God and with one another. God has loved us, does love us, and will love us faithfully. In the same way, we should love God and one another.

Jesus said to love God and love your neighbor as yourself. We should be concerned about others' needs and feelings without discounting our own. Physical intimacy can be as simple as a handshake or a hug, or as total as the intimacy of marriage. Sometimes we ask, What is the right kind of intimacy? We must remember that sexual intercourse should be reserved for marriage.

Some people say responsible sexual behavior is simply a matter of following rules for right and wrong. Other people say it is an individual matter of deciding for yourself what is right and wrong. Our understanding of responsible sexuality is not found at either of these two extremes. We are part of the community of faith. Joined together, we read and study God's Word, pray and listen for God's guidance for us, study the beliefs of our church in the past, and then—being guided by all this—we make statements together that express our beliefs. We take definite stands on issues. At the same time, we uphold the right of each person to maintain the dignity of his or her conscience in the light of the Scriptures.

We know that God's Spirit is present when there is love, joy, peace, patience, kindness, goodness, fidelity, gentleness, and self-control. We can be sure that we are acting responsibly when we keep God's Spirit as the guide of our lives.

Decision-Making Guide*

Step 1: What is the decision to be made?

Step 2: What are three possible solutions?

1.

2.

3.

Step 3: What have my family, church, and friends said about the choices that I need to consider?

Step 4: What would be the positive and the negative results of each solution?

Solution 1 (from above)
Positive Results   *Negative Results*

Solution 2 (from above)
Positive Results   *Negative Results*

Solution 3 (from above)
Positive Results   *Negative Results*

Step 5: Compare all the alternatives, make a choice, and write down your choice here.

Step 6: What steps need to be taken to carry out this choice?

*Used with permission from *Life Skills and Opportunities* (Philadelphia: Public/Private Ventures, 1987).

Decision-Making Guide Dilemmas

Dilemma 1: Tony and Sara are growing in their relationship. They are very attracted to each other, and when they are alone they get so sexually excited that they both feel out of control. What should they do?

Dilemma 2: Robert feels bad about himself because he wants to wait until marriage to have sex. According to his friends, the movies, and television, he is the only person in the world who feels this way. He is rethinking his beliefs and wonders whether he perhaps would have sex before marriage if the right girl were to come along. What should he do?

Dilemma 3: Jamaal's parents are not sure that a thirteen-year-old should be dating. Jamaal wants to go out on a double date with his brother, who can drive. What should his parents do?

Dilemma 4: Maria's boyfriend wants her to look at sex magazines with him. She feels uncomfortable and embarrassed; he keeps insisting. What should she do?

Dilemma 5: Kumiko is interested in going with Mark, but he has not paid much attention to her. Her friends say she has to wait until he calls her. Can she make the first move? What should she do?

Litany for Decision Makers

Leader: O God, you have made us responsible.

Group: Responsible to you.

Leader: We are responsible to you, God, for the decisions we make.

Group: But decision making is hard.

Leader: We want to do what is right, what you want us to do, God.

Group: But we hear other voices.

Girls: Friends.

Boys: Television.

Girls: Magazines.

Boys: Music.

Group: And the voices are so loud!

Leader: Help us, God, to stand for what is right. Help us to make good decisions.

Group: And forgive us when we mess up.

Leader: You have given us choices, O God.

Group: Help us be responsible decision makers. Amen.

So You Think You Know Your Parent(s)?

Teen Worksheet

You probably think you know your parent(s) pretty well. After all, you probably see him or her almost every day. But there may be a lot you don't know. This activity will help you realize how much—or how little—you know your parent(s).

   Directions: Answer these questions. At the same time, your mother or father (stepmother or stepfather) will answer the questions on "So You Think You Know Your Teen?" When you are finished, exchange and correct each other's worksheets.

1. What color are your mom's/dad's eyes?

2. What is your mom's/dad's favorite restaurant?

3. How would your mom/dad describe their work?

4. What kind of music did your mom/dad listen to when they were your age?

5. When visiting a big city, would your mom/dad rather visit a museum, attend a sporting event, go shopping, or dine in a fancy restaurant?

6. Which room of the house does your mom/dad prefer to spend time in?

7. Would your mom/dad rather drive a truck, a sports car, a station wagon, or a luxury car?

8. What type of movie does your mom/dad like best: action, comedy, or romance?

9. Who is your mom's/dad's closest friend?

10. Did your mom/dad have a favorite childhood pet?

11. What does your mom/dad like to eat for breakfast?

12. If your mom/dad could visit any country in the world, which one would it be?

   Note: In the future, you and your parent(s) might enjoy making up your own questions for this activity. You also might want to take this test every few months so you don't lose track of the details of your parent's life. *Remember:* Knowing or wanting to find out about someone shows that you truly care. What's more, it can be fun.

Better Communication—Word Choice

When we communicate with others, the words we use can mean the difference between getting our point across clearly and making someone feel hurt, angry, or rejected. This activity is designed to help you find better ways to communicate with your child or parent.

Directions: The sentences that follow are examples of poor word choice. Parents and children should take turns reading these sentences and discussing your reactions to them.

Parent: I just can't trust you.
Youth: You never let me do anything.
Parent: You never do what I say.
Youth: You're so old-fashioned. Everyone is doing it.
Parent: I can't believe you did that.
Youth: You never trust me.

Parents

Write down something your son or daughter says that gets a negative reaction from you.

My son/daughter says: _____

_____
_____
_____
_____ .

Discuss this statement with him/her, and then reword it to make it more effective communication.

I'd rather hear my son/daughter say: _____

_____
_____
_____
_____ .

Youth

Write down something your parent says that gets a negative reaction from you.

My mom/dad says: _____

_____
_____
_____
_____ .

Discuss this statement with your mom or dad and then reword it to make it more effective communication.

I'd rather hear my mom/dad say: _____

_____
_____
_____
_____ .

Messages about Sex

Teen Worksheet

Your parents are the most important educators and role models for human sexuality that you will have. However—despite their best intentions—the messages they send are often not the same as the ones you receive. This activity will help you be sure the messages you get from your parent or parents about sexuality are the messages they intend to give.

Directions: Complete this worksheet while your parent or parents do theirs. Write three messages your parent(s) have given you about sex. These messages may be actual statements they have made, such as "Sex should be a private act." They may be messages about sex that you haven't actually heard your parent(s) say, but think they believe. Or they may be messages you've received from observing your parent's lives and relationships.

1.

2.

3.

After you and your parent(s) have written three messages on your worksheets, get together and read the messages you have written. Ask your parent(s) whether these are the messages he or she intended to give. If so, discuss whether you have clearly and completely understood the messages. If they are not messages your parent(s) meant to give, discuss why you perceived them in this way and find out how the misunderstood message differs from your parent's actual beliefs.

Litany

People: God did a curious thing when we were created. Sometimes it is hard to understand that God made us so different. Girls' behavior is different from boys' behavior and boys' behavior is different from girls' behavior, and all this is part of sexuality. From the beginning, sexuality has been a part of God's creation. God created us as sexual beings—to be boys and girls, men and women.

Leader: So this curious thing that God has done becomes a tremendous experience—our experience! Scripture says that when God made male and female, man and woman, God said, "It is good."

People: It *is* good—it is great! Our sexuality, our femaleness and maleness, is who we are. It is what we will be. We are turned loose to think, talk, and decide.

Leader: It makes us feel strange to be so free. There is so much we want to know. Thinking of God and sex at the same time and saying both in the same breath reminds us of how all love comes from one source.

People: It makes us feel good. We want to think, talk, know, and be the best girl or boy, man or woman, we can be. We want to use the gift of our sexuality to its fullest.

Leader: Praise God that we are sexual beings. Right?

People: Right!

Leader: Thank God that we are free to discover, examine, and decide.

People: Right!

Leader: Amen.

People: And Amen.

Sexuality Course Evaluation

Youth

I would rate the sexuality education course as:

UNINTERESTING	SLIGHTLY INTERESTING	OK	GOOD	GREAT
☐	☐	☐	☐	☐

The most interesting part of the course was:

The thing I enjoyed most about the course was:

The thing I enjoyed least about the course was:

The part of the course most important to me was:

I wish there had been more:

Other comments: